a blind salmon

A Blind Salmon

Julia Wong Kcomt

Translated by Jennifer Shyue

PHONEME MEDIA | DEEP VELLUM

DALLAS, TEXAS

Phoneme Media, an imprint of Deep Vellum Publishing
3000 Commerce St., Dallas, Texas 75226
deepvellum.org · @deepvellum

Deep Vellum is a 501c3 nonprofit literary arts organization founded in 2013 with the
mission to bring the world into conversation through literature.

Support for this publication has been provided in part by grants from the National Endow-
ment for the Arts, the Texas Commission on the Arts, the City of Dallas Office of Arts and
Culture, the Communities Foundation of Texas, and the Addy Foundation.

ISBN: 978-1-64605-306-3 (paperback) | ISBN: 978-1-64605-321-6 (ebook)

LIBRARY OF CONGRESS CATALOGING-IN-PUBLICATION DATA:

Names: Wong Kcomt, Julia, author. | Shyue, Jennifer, translator. | Wong
Kcomt, Julia. Blind salmon. | Wong Kcomt, Julia. Blind salmon. Spanish
Title: A blind salmon / Julia Wong Kcomt ; translated by Jennifer Shyue.
Other titles: Blind salmon (Compilation)
Description: First edition. | Dallas, Texas : Deep Vellum, 2024.
Identifiers: LCCN 2023056561 (print) | LCCN 2023056562 (ebook) | ISBN
9781646053063 (paperback) | ISBN 9781646053216 (e-book)
Subjects: LCSH: Wong Kcomt, Julia--Translations into English. | LCGFT:
Poetry.
Classification: LCC PQ8498.433.O54 B5813 2024 (print) | LCC PQ8498.433.O54
(ebook) | DDC 861/.7--dc23/eng/20240105
LC record available at https://lccn.loc.gov/2023056561
LC ebook record available at https://lccn.loc.gov/2023056562

Cover design by Sarah Schulte
Interior layout and typesetting by KGT

PRINTED IN CANADA

CONTENTS

armenian rose   9

song of the multiform bird   11

potrero de santa rosa   15

manners   19

gabriella sleeps   23

there were things in buenos aires   25

the desert dispels   27

on sameness   29

aunt emma doesn't want to die   33

tijuana big margarita   39

dark jasmines. jazmines negros   43

lagoon on calle rodríguez peña   45

the blind salmon   47

natural blood   51

cajamarca   53

a feather falls   57

i ought to go live in colombia   59

the cultural code of the sand   63

manicure   67

poem on distance   67

rhapsody of the tiger   73

on sameness   75

why do your differences   79

my guardian angel   83

opium weddings   87

the war   91

madness on the highest building   103

chernobyl kid   107

i want to kill my sister   109

poem for georg trakl   111

mother and daughter   115

by the river   119

woman eaten by cats   123

Translator's Afterword by Jennifer Shyue   125

Translator's Acknowledgments   129

Biographical Information   131

For Ceci Abad, Patricia Cuaranta, and Carlos Amézaga

rosa de armenia

muchacha de cuatro días
mueres en las uñas sucias
de un hambriento
des-
hojando
una niña
un tul blanco
unas caderas anchas como tu país
destrozado tu país
tu cielo
tu sol

y sin embargo de cada espina
bordas otra flor
y en cada beso reconstruyes
al maligno hiriéndote en la espalda
pidiéndote
que escondas toda, toda tu belleza
con inocente sabia lucidez,
escapaste.

armenian rose

little girl, four days old, you go
lifeless in the grimy nails of
a starving man
shu-
cking petals off
a girl
pale tulle
pair of hips wide as your country
your country wrecked
your sky
and sun

and nevertheless with every thorn
you embroider another flower
and in every kiss you reconstruct
the malignancy wounding your back
that asks you
to obscure it all, all your beauty
with innocent wise lucidity,
you escaped.

canción del pájaro multiforme

el padre de mi hija era mejicano
y yo le tengo miedo a esa frontera
más que al sol y sus manchas glandulares
más que a un tsunami

y me pregunto si la sangre es de barbarie o solo de reclamo
que me entiendas, pide la sangre
que me tomes, ruega
por eso entre cruces, adobes y bajopuentes
más incomprensible es el desierto
voraz

y como mujer hacia la santidad no debería hablar de vergas
ni adulterio
pero fiel a mí misma
quisiera comer los restos de palabras
que eielson dejó en las traspuertas
el pelo negro del homo sapiens
escrito sobre polvo acumulado

qué pena que se me haya terminado la vergüenza
y llore como una loca
cuando un perro se caga en mi puerta

me enternece la calle sedienta de pascuas
las mesas con mucha gente
la humillación de los crueles
la gomina

song of the multiform bird

my daughter's father was mejicano
and i fear that border
more than the sun and its glandular splotches
more than a tsunami

and i wonder whether this blood is savagery or just grievance
understand me: the blood's request
drink me, it pleads
which is why, between crosses, adobe, and skyways
the hardest to understand is the ravenous
desert

and since i'm a woman turned toward saintliness i shouldn't
    talk of cocks
or adultery
but i, faithful to myself
would like to eat the remains of words
eielson left at the ledge
black hair of homo sapiens
scrawled on piled dust

it's a pity i no longer have shame
and i weep like a madwoman
when a dog shits at my door

i am softened by the parched easter street
the tables full of people
the humiliation of the cruel
the hair gel

y me pregunto si mi hija
ya entendió que es un pájaro sin fronteras
mató a su padre en medio de un bolero amurallado
me hirió de muerte
para que la deje ser alondra
perdiz
huaba madura
incorregible cactus en pakatnamú

y me dijo
que hay palabras que trae en sus células
que yo nunca entendería
que entre su nariz y la mía por más amor
por más amor
no puedo abrazarla.

and i wonder whether my daughter
now understands she's a borderless bird
who killed her father during a walled-in bolero
wounded me fatally
so i'd let her be a lark
partridge
ripe huaba
incorrigible cactus in pakatnamú

and she said
her cells contained words
i would never understand
that between her nose and mine
for all the love
for all the love
i'm not allowed to hold her.

potrero de santa rosa

no he podido completar el dibujo de la flor
ni el de la casa
el cigarro se quedó prendido en el cenicero

carraspeo
tamborileo en la mesa
no vendrán a comer, ya es tarde

hice pudín de maicena
humitas envueltas en hojas de oliva
un guiso de choclo
el vino es bueno

uno se ha quedado mirando el firmamento
la otra llora a su hijo muerto

qué pasó con las tres estrellas que papá dibujaba en la arena
fuimos solo agua
estrellas de agua
diluidas en carmín: un sueño
anoche recordé como
saludábamos a los barcos que no podían vernos de vuelta
mi hermano llevaba un bastón y decía
síganme

después cada cual siguió un camino pintado con leche
o con sangre
y ahora se nos ha prohibido el habla
porque contamos cosas que nadie ha visto
porque rogamos a un dios que nadie conoce

potrero de santa rosa

i haven't been able to finish drawing the flower
or the house
the cigarette's still lit in the ashtray

i clear my throat
drum fingers on the table
they're not coming to dinner, it's too late

i made corn pudding
humitas wrapped in olive leaves
a choclo stew
the wine is good

one stares at the firmament
the other cries to her dead son

what happened to the three stars papá drew in the sand
we were just water
watery stars
diluted in carmine: a dream
last night i remembered how
we waved at ships that couldn't see us
my brother carried a walking stick and said
follow me

after, each of us followed a path dappled with milk
or blood
and now we are forbidden to speak
because we tell of things no one's seen
because we plead to a god no one knows

porque éramos felices los tres juntos

no sé dónde está mi hermano
y escucho que mi hermana llora y sigue y sigue llorando
yo también grito detrás de la puerta y nadie escucha

no supimos hacer un mundo nuevo
alguien nos hizo y deshizo a su manera
mis hermanos
mis hermanos.

because we were happy together, us three

i don't know where my brother is
and i hear my sister crying and she keeps and she keeps crying
and i too scream behind the door and no one hears

we didn't know how to make a new world
someone made and unmade us in their way
my brother and sister
my brother and sister.

educación

ella enseña, mírala
mira su boca pintada de rojo
así se hace, dice
obedezco

una porción de arroz con queso de soya
(no sé comer ese arroz)
tan diferente al de casa, tan diferente el olor de estas mandarinas
las nueces de corazón abierto
las que pela mamá están llenas de manchas y arrugas negras

un hombre feliz se acerca a mamá y la saluda
hablemos de china, dice
canta y hace una mueca oportuna
estos retoños
hombres del mañana, tez de porcelana

varias veces veo gente que aparece sin cabeza y el espíritu
desbocado
gente enojada
comprando jades de plástico, comiendo
moviéndose
quiero estar con mi mamá cuando me entra esta pena

es una pena grande
un corazón cargado de no sé que
quisiera que mamá me explique por qué hay niños hablando
algo que no entiendo
por qué tengo que hablar algo que no entiendo

manners

she's teaching, look at her
look at her red-varnished mouth
this is how, she says
i obey

one serving of rice with bean curd
(i have no idea how to eat this rice)
so different from home, the smell of these mandarins so different
these open-heart nuts
the ones mamá peels are splotched, crinkled, and black

a happy man comes up to greet mamá
let's talk about china, he says
he sings and makes a proper face
these little ones
tomorrow's men, skin of porcelain

a couple times i see people who appear without heads, spirits
running loose
angry people
buying jade made of plastic, eating
moving
i want to be with mamá when that sadness overtakes me

it's a big sadness
a heart loaded with who knows what
i'd like mamá to tell me why there are children saying
things i don't understand
why i have to say things i don't understand

miras las calles, se tornan diferentes con puertas rojas
y edificios raros, antes todas eran casas comunes
ahora vive gente que viene de tan lejos
del reino del centro, fuego del mundo
superstición
el aire tiembla
dos patos pekineses pronostican mucha prosperidad
extraño a mi mamá y mi papá está preparando algo dulce

maestra de chino
quiero llorar, mis mejillas aguantadas
cuando quiera marcharme de este lugar
¿cómo hará usted para mantener el lápiz
dibujando una montaña entristecida?

you look at the streets, they've transformed with red doors
and strange buildings, before these were all regular houses
now the people who live here come from so far
from the middle kingdom, fire of the world
superstition
the air trembles
two peking ducks predict much prosperity
i miss mamá and papá is making something sweet

ms. chinese teacher
i want to cry, my cheeks stifled
when i decide to leave this place
what will you do to keep my pencil
drawing a grieving mountain?

gabriella duerme
marejada incólume
gabriella grita
marejada en la ingle
gabriella me pide que no tenga sexo con nadie

sé mi manantial mamá reclaman sus ojos
la piscina eterna
para esa cola de sirena en la ciudad
grita

el torrente loco
mar hablando
palabras
palabras
de pájaros cometas
palabras

gabriella es la última palabra del cuerpo.

gabriella sleeps
an impervious swell
gabriella screams
swell in the groin
gabriella asks me not to have sex with anyone

be my wellspring mamá her eyes insist
eternal pool
for that mermaid tail in the city
she screams

the mad torrent
sea speaking
words
words
of kite birds
words

gabriella is the body's last word.

habían cosas en buenos aires
como las hojas aplastadas cerca a un cine sobre rivadavia
como un pedazo de almendro norteño muerto
en la calle

habían pedazos de palabras que se habían caído de maletines
    rosados
de cabezas de elefantes peruanos, de esos aparecidos
en la calle rodríguez peña, donde borges iba a leer periódico

y yo pensaba que era entre algodón y realidad subterránea dejar
que un hombre de ojos azules
apareciera y se fuera corriendo
y yo le.decía
esta boca está sangrando, pero se ha secado
y él decía
así es buenos aires, así es.

there were things in buenos aires
like the crumpled leaves next to the theater on rivadavia
like a piece of northern almond tree dead
in the street

pieces of words fallen from pink briefcases
from the heads of peruvian elephants, from the apparitions
on calle rodríguez peña, where borges went to read the paper

and i thought it'd be something between cotton and underground
    reality to let
a blue-eyed man
appear and take off at a run
and i told him
this mouth is bleeding, but it has dried
and he said
that's buenos aires, yes.

el desierto ahuyenta este campo sagrado de insinuaciones burdas, complejo de ciudad, de alma humana queriendo abigarrarse en hierro, cemento, vitrales, ósculos de santos, mosaicos medioevales.

el desierto trae esa capa de infinito, color entre blanco y carne, entre beige y canela untada en el horizonte; entrega pensamientos claros, arena en la boca, una incomodidad casi necesaria para recrear el aura gloriosa de una mente feliz, tranquila, disipada, que todo lo puede albergar y digerir como bocado preciso.

el desierto descascara las uñas mordidas, mal pintadas, entre un caos de ama de casa aburrida, zapallos mal pelados, baldes rotos, jabón para pisos. me vuelve a imagen y semejanza de la música que solo acaricia la limpieza de la vista, la sangre volviéndose arena. dunas y dunas, las palabras. pasos en el silencio, sin ambigüedad. un temple de voluntad bien utilizado, como si no se necesitara moral, ni historia entre los movimientos agrarios donde la dimensión de castidad se pierde en la urbe chorreando café, cigarrillos, amazonas peleando la moda, los cosméticos, la mirada incólume de la plasticidad.

el desierto en tu ojo.
el desierto en mi mano.
el desierto caliente y frío.

el desierto en la noche tibia, en la oreja dispuesta de una abeja reina que prepara el último aguijón de la batalla.

un par de alas inventadas surcan el corolario del crepúsculo. el desierto mengua la ira, acicala el veneno y soy invento del cielo, soy nube soplada. fulmino con mi amor toda la calle, soy ballena.

the desert dispels this hallowed ground of coarse insinuations,
complex of city, of human soul wishing to daub itself in iron, cement,
stained glass, saintly osculations, medieval mosaics.

the desert brings that infinite layer, its color between white and flesh,
between beige and cinnamon smeared on the horizon; it delivers clear
thoughts, sand in mouth, a discomfort almost necessary to recreate the
glorious aura of a happy, calm, dissolute mind, capable of harboring it all
and digesting it, precise mouthful.

the desert flays the chewed nails, sloppy polished, among the chaos of a
bored housewife, poorly peeled squash, broken buckets, soap for floors. it
returns me to image and likeness of the music brushing against the clean-
ing of view, blood turning to sand. dunes and dunes, those words. foot-
steps in the silence, unambiguous. a tempering of well-used will, as if no
morals were needed, nor history between the agrarian movements in
which chastity's standing was lost in the metropolis oozing coffee, cig-
arettes, amazons struggling fashion, cosmetics, the impervious gaze of
plasticity.

the desert in your eye.
the desert in my hand.
the desert cold and hot.

the desert on a mild night, in the ready ear of a queen bee preparing the
battle's final stinger.

a pair of fabricated wings furrow dusk's repercussions. the desert shrinks
rage, burnishes poison and i'm the sky's fabrication, i'm a blown-up
cloud. with my love i strike down the whole street, i am a whale.

on sameness

in the circle, sweet circle
of intense immortality

where is my china?
the land with no owners
the face is not repeating itself

the voices are a drum changing the way the sun flies

the perspicacity of the five senses
five streets
five calamities

but the west eye
have more intentions than faces, they will fill
the chinese emptiness with
anger and cruel desires

the shell egg it's broken
that's not love, not a epic intention
how can a cross in a kiev's beautiful church
run down a south american river

a kind of desperation
who is fucking whom
who is crying the bloody waves
of a shacked pacific ocean

i don't want to move
don't want a dog
don't need a maid

on sameness

in the circle, sweet circle
of intense immortality

where is my china?
the land with no owners
the face is not repeating itself

the voices are a drum changing the way the sun flies

the perspicacity of the five senses
five streets
five calamities

but the west eye
has more intentions than faces, they will fill
the chinese emptiness with
anger and cruel desires

the shell egg it's broken
that's not love, not a epic intention
how can a cross in a kiev's beautiful church
run down a south american river

a kind of desperation
who is fucking whom
who is crying the bloody waves
of a shacked pacific ocean

i don't want to move
don't want a dog
don't need a maid

don't need the imagination
of a southern goodness

the colors of water
peter's beautiful eyes still move my heart
some days with pavlo made me happy
and the street's corner after forty three years
it's the house of the beginning

i was born in this city
this city almost conquered my soul
i want to keep my mother alive forever
i want my brother and my sister back en el potrero
de santa rosa.

don't need the imagination
of a southern goodness

the colors of water
peter's beautiful eyes still move my heart
some days with pavlo made me happy
and the street's corner after forty three years
it's the house of the beginning

i was born in this city
this city almost conquered my soul
i want to keep my mother alive forever
i want my brother and my sister back en el potrero
de santa rosa.

tía emma no quiere morir

no sé cómo despedirme. me preocupa que pases la noche sola y te quedes con ganas de seguir contando sobre tus viajes. cuando salgo de tu casa y dejo que la luz del crepúsculo me acompañe hasta la parada de autobús, me confundo entre culpa y desolación, también me apacigua haber pasado un buen rato juntas. quisiera sentir lástima por tus manos, supongo que te duelen, mas no la tengo. admiro tus manos, me apena que ya no puedas tocar piano, ni hacer tortas de crema como las hacía tu abuela en viena. ya no necesitas ni tocar el piano, ni hacer tortas. tu mirada se extravía, cuando yo limpio las teclas en desuso y, mientras me observas, parecieras sentir cierta nostalgia irresistible; sé que solo es un momento dramático de recuerdos, luego sabes que aun teniendo los dedos sanos, ya no tocarías, prefieres regar tus orquídeas y leer libros con ilustraciones, mirar la tarde marcharse por la ventana y recibir amigas que te cuenten lo que pasa en el pueblo.

tienes una enorme foto en sepia de la casa vieja de viena colgada en el salón. tampoco la miras, se quedó allí para que todos sepan de donde vienes. knittlingen se volvió tu ciudad, te enamoraste de la plaza, de cada calle, del cielo, de los jardines; pero sobre todo te enamoraste del restaurante, de la cocina grande, de las cacerolas, los spaetzle, los dampfnudeln y la salsa de vainilla.

no hubo nada mejor que trabajar y atender a los comensales. así te olvidabas de juergen y de aquella unión imposible. sé que sabes que aún lloro a escondidas. sé que presientes mi tristeza cuando pienso en reiner. las dos estamos entrelazadas por una maldita coincidencia. tu gran amor fue el marido de tu prima hermana y yo me enamoré perdidamente de un muchacho que nunca se fijaría en mí.

aunt emma doesn't want to die

i don't know how to say goodbye. i'm worried that you'll be alone all
night with stories still to tell about your trips. as i leave your house and let
the day's last light accompany me to the bus stop, i waver between guilt
and anguish. it does make me feel better that we spent a good amount of
time together. i wish i could feel pity for your hands—i'm guessing they
hurt—but i don't. i admire them, it makes me sad you can't play piano
anymore, or make cream cakes like the ones your grandmother in vienna
made. you no longer need to play piano, or make cakes. your gaze wan-
ders while i clean the untouched keys, and as you observe what i'm doing,
you seem to feel a certain irresistible nostalgia; i know it's just a dramatic
moment of reminiscing, then you realize that even if your fingers could
still do it, you prefer watering your orchids or reading illustrated books,
observing as the afternoon passes by your window, and hosting girl-
friends who tell you what's happening in town.

in the living room hangs a huge sepia photo of the old vienna house.
you don't look at that either, it's there so everyone will know where
you're from. knittlingen became your city, you fell in love with the main
square, with every street, the sky, the gardens; but most of all, you fell in
love with the restaurant, the big kitchen, the casseroles, the spaetzle, the
dampfnudeln, and the vanilla sauce.

there was nothing better than working and looking after the guests. you
could forget about juergen and that impossible union. i know you know
that sometimes i still cry in secret. i know you sense how sad i get when
i think about reiner. you and i are linked by a cursed coincidence. your
great love married your cousin, and i fell hopelessly in love with a guy
who would never notice me.

sabes que me contagiaste la pasión por los viajes. sí, ya sé que todos los alemanes viajan y viajan como buscando sol, otra luz, mejor comida o mejores ofertas a cualquier rincón exótico del planeta. pero el placer de viajar a ti te venía por otro lado. por esas ganas de descubrir, de admirar la belleza de los otros. me parecía surreal que hubieras tomado el té con indira gandhi y que hubieran charlado más de diez minutos sobre política internacional, no es que tú supieras mucho, pero tu porte, tu sonrisa, provocaba tanto respeto y confidencialidad, que el mismo mao te hubiera contado sus estrategias de guerra.

reiner tenía una foto con un tigre en kenya, me fascinó desde que lo vi. como un maniquí perfecto de tienda. tenía la quijada partida y unos ojos tremendamente bellos. me dijiste. ni lo mires margarita. él no es para ti. ¿cómo no lo iba a mirar tía emma?, reiner y el tigre entraron retozando en mi vida y se quedaron como si yo los hubiera enjaulado. no, ellos me enjaularon a mí.

no sé ni cómo llegué a tu casa. pediste una *au pair* a la agencia, para que cuidara a los hijos de la hermana de reiner, pero gudrun era alérgica a la piel morena y a la gente que no fuera europea.

no soportó mi locuacidad, mis nervios latinoamericanos. yo ya estaba en knittlingen, entusiasmada por haber conseguido un trabajo en europa. te apiadaste, cambiaste todo el contrato y me pediste como dama de compañía. de paso me pagaste los estudios de alemán y me animaste a inscribirme en la fachhochschule para estudiar turismo. al principio viví contigo, en tu pulcra casa, junto a tus libros de viajes, tus recuerdos, tu piano y las recetas del restaurante que fuera de tu familia. "especialidades vienesas". la vida se te iba, querías hacer algo contundente y grandioso por alguien que casi estuviera desahuciado por el sistema económico. no para que te agradezca, eras demasiado generosa para eso. te gusté. también me gustaste. eras una dama muy fina, de sonrisa angelical y mirada profunda. cuando miré a reiner y el tigre, me pediste que me fuera.

you know you infected me with a passion for travel. yes, i'm well aware
that all germans travel as if searching for sun, other light, better food, or
better deals, traveling to any of the planet's exotic corners. but you got
the pleasure of travel from something else. from that desire to discover,
to admire other people's beauty. it's surreal to me that you had tea with
indira gandhi and chatted with her for over ten minutes about interna-
tional policy; it's not that you knew so much, but your bearing, your
smile inspired such confidence and respect that mao himself would've
told you his military strategies.

there was a photo of reiner with a tiger in kenya. i've found it fascinat-
ing ever since i saw it. he's a perfect store mannequin with a cleft chin and
gorgeous eyes. you told me. no looking, margarita. he's not for you. how
could i not look, aunt emma? reiner and the tiger capered into my life and
then stayed like i'd put them in a cage. no, they were the ones who put me
in a cage.

i don't even know how i came to be at your house. you requested an au
pair from the agency, to care for reiner's sister's children, but gudrun was
allergic to dark skin and non-europeans. she couldn't stand my chatti-
ness, my latin nerves. i was already in knittlingen, excited to have found
work in europe. you took pity, revised the contract, and requested me as
your caretaker. you also paid for my german classes and encouraged me
to enroll at the fachhochschule to study tourism. at first i lived with you,
in your meticulous house, among your travelogues, your memories, your
piano, and the recipes from your family's restaurant. "viennese special-
ties." life was passing you by, you wanted to do something impactful, a big
gesture, for someone whom the economic system had stripped of almost
all hope. not so they'd be grateful, you were too generous for that. you
liked me. i liked you too. you were a fine lady, with an angelic smile and
a deep gaze. when i started making eyes at reiner and the tiger, you asked
me to leave.

tenía una habitación muy pequeña en la vivienda de estudiantes. estudiaba cuatro horas diarias, cuidaba niños otras cuatro y luego iba para tu casa. mirábamos fotos. me contabas de viena, también de la guerra. un tema absurdo. yo estaba preocupada por enamorarme de alguien y tú por olvidar algo. aquella guerra entre ustedes no me importaba. no la comprendía.

no me querías mirar cuando me mudé. desconozco ese sentimiento en las latitudes geográficas de donde vengo ¿se llama vergüenza étnica?, perpetuación del folclore.

reiner era la fruta prohibida junto al tigre de kenya y tú me odiaste porque yo la mordí aquella noche de luna llena cuando bailaban disfrazados los niños en la plaza.

nunca debiste hacerlo, me dijiste. era grande tu ira. yo tu protegida, cometía el peor de los crímenes para tus ojos pulcros, purísimos, cada vez menos radiantes, pero esperanzados en un corazón caliente como el mío. tienes que irte a la vivienda de estudiantes —sentenciaste.

y aunque equivocadamente pensé que reiner me buscaría o llamaría, eso no sucedió. tampoco hubiera sido necesario. su torso se quedó grabado en mi ingle. la piel puede resultar una suerte de memoria reproductora.

en la vivienda de estudiantes otra vez estaba rodeada de gente como yo. extranjeros. qué difícil ser extraño, venir de afuera, pelear, robar, hacer de todo para ser de adentro y los de adentro tiran el anzuelo y luego lo quitan.

yo tenía el cuerpo roto, agujereado de todas las veces que la foto de reiner me horadó hasta que se colaron los ojos cuestionadores de tía emma. llena de huecos dejé de pensar que alemania me acogería como propia algún día.

i had a very small room in student housing. i was in school for four hours a day, looked after children for another four, and then i went to your house. we leafed through photos. you told me about vienna, and about the war. an absurd topic. i was preoccupied with falling in love with someone and you with forgetting something. that war of yours didn't matter to me. i didn't understand it.

when i was moving out, you wouldn't look at me. at the geographic latitudes i'm from, we're unfamiliar with that feeling. is it called ethnic guilt? perpetuation of folklore.

reiner was the forbidden fruit next to the tiger from kenya and you hated me because i took a bite that full-moon night as the children danced in costumes in the square.

you should never have done that, you told me. you were so angry. i, your protégée, had committed the worst crime in your eyes, your eyes so meticulous, pure, increasingly dim, but hopeful, with a heart that ran hot like mine. you must go live in student housing, you decreed.

and though i thought reiner would come looking for me or call me, that didn't happen. not that it would've been necessary. his torso had imprinted on my groin. sometimes skin serves as a sort of reproduction.

in student housing i was once again surrounded by people like me. foreigners. it's so hard to be a stranger, to come from elsewhere, to fight, to steal, to do anything to get inside and the insiders throw you bait only to take it away.

my body was broken, poked full of holes from all the times reiner's photo perforated me until aunt emma's questioning eyes crept in. pocked, i stopped thinking that germany would one day accept me as its own.

tijuana gran margarita

destrózame línea, la
línea
ráyame en ese vacío buscando ciudades
línea
ni de aquí, tampoco de allá
edificios de caracoles
palmeras
de ají
caras redondas, cuerpos como roperos
maíz y hambre
norte, lejano, línea, ráyame de nuevo
sur y norte
norte y panzas huecas
llenas de shopping malls
línea ráyame la cara
línea
píntame
ni de abajo ni de arriba
crúzame
from dawn till dusk
the geographic proportions of desperation

miss america is gone to tijuana
píntale un corazoncito de mariachi
en una pista solitaria
llena de muertos mojados

black fat woman drive my car
far from this line

tijuana big margarita

wreck me línea, the
línea
slash me in that void seeking cities
línea
not from here, or there
seashell buildings
palm trees
of ají
round faces, bodies like armoires
corn and hunger
north, far, línea, slash me
again
south and north
north and hollow bellies
full of shopping malls
línea slash me in the face
línea
paint me
not from below or above
cross me
desde el amanecer hasta el anochecer
las proporciones geográficas de la desesperación
miss america fue a tijuana
paint her a little mariachi heart
on a lonesome highway
full of soaked corpses

negra gorda
conduce mi carro
lejos de esta línea

no soy aquí, ni allá
pero sigo siendo
la r e i
n
a

donde se juntan todas las veredas tropicales
elmusgolasalverjaselmolelapimienta
unbesodehombremorenoporelsoldelcarmen.

i am neither here, nor there
but still i remain
la r e i
n
a

where all the tropical paths meet
themossthepeasthemolethepepper
akissfromadarkmanforthesunovercarmen.

jazmines negros. dark jazmines

la lluvia es un gendarme ciego
me despierta y protege
tenue

la vida va y viene como agua
dura un año
diez, setenta
u ochentai . . . (no, no lo digas)

la vida es una llamada por teléfono
¿estás bien mamá?
¿estás contenta?

su rictus facial desmejoraba
cuando el agua de mi cerebro
se hacía muñeca de papel

hay noches que solo
las salva el sudor
y el encierro

el grito de amor
es lo que esconden mis ayunos
los países conquistados

me desgarro mamá
no quería que lo escuches.

dark jasmines. jazmines negros

the rain is a blind gendarme
it awakens and protects me
so faint

life comes and goes like water
lasts a year
ten, seventy
or eighty- . . . (no, don't say it)

life is a phone call
are you OK mamá?
are you happy?

her wincing sagged
when the water surrounding my brain
became a paper doll

there are nights when the only thing
saving them is the sweat
and confinement

love's shrieks
are what my fasts hide
the conquered countries

i'm ripping apart mamá
i didn't want you to hear.

albufera de la calle rodríguez peña

como un río
alguna parte de tu cadera es una quebrada
en mi boca seca

lamo un dulce de miel apelmazado
antiguo, repitiéndose
tan siniestro
vuelve a ser liquen
fluido, mar

soy una flor técnica de las siete de la mañana
albufera de siesta
mientras como, no me diluyo
las olas se marchan
revientan
vendedores de nardos, de autos, de gente diestra
entre granos de sal adormecidas
fuego de ciudad
en los baños lluvia escondida

el café promisorio
las gargantas fumando
viviré un día más en buenos aires, lo prometo.

lagoon on calle rodríguez peña

like a river
some part of your hip
is a ravine
in my dry mouth

i'm licking a piece of dense honey candy
ancient, repeating
so sinisterly
turning back to lichen
fluid, sea

i am a technical bloom at seven in the morning
siesta lagoon
as i eat, i do not dilute
the waves retreat
burst
vendors of tuberoses, cars, right-handers
among grains of drowsing salt
city fire
in the baths, hidden rain

promissory coffee
throats lighting up a smoke
i'll live another day in buenos aires, i promise.

el salmón ciego

calma
calma
alrededor no solo hay agua y sucedáneos de matriz, ya lo sé

mis escamas
un libro de profecías no cumplidas
ojos hinchados
ojeras de judío enhiesto

nado, miro y no miro
nado
nunca he vuelto a ver
a un hombre con las manos de sabio, derrumbando
                   ídolos y pidiendo de rodillas

vuelve sol
fertiliza los huevecillos

nada me hará nadar hacia otro mar. esta agua, la bebo, la rebebo
la respiro
la sudan mis branquias
excreto la baba de mis amistades pasajeras

no, no veo quién es más grande que yo
me deleito en mi propia pulpa
y mis ojos callan
y mi boca sigue tragando más aire del que necesito
quiero reventar
entre madera y oxígeno
calma
soy el salmón moreno, agujereado

the blind salmon

quiet
quiet
this isn't just water and womb substitute, i know

my scales
a book of unfulfilled prophecies
swollen eyes
purple circles of an upstanding jew

i swim, i look and don't
i swim
never again did i see
a man with a sage's hands, toppling
       idols and begging on his knees

come back sun
fertilize the little eggs

nothing can make me swim to other seas. this water, i drink it, redrink it
i breathe it
it sweats from my gills
i secrete the spit from my fleeting friendships

no, i can't see who's bigger than me
i delight in my own pulp
and my eyes hush
and my mouth keeps gulping more air than i need
i want to burst
between wood and oxygen
quiet
i am a dark-skinned salmon, poked full of holes

nunca pescado
desierto
norte del techo del mundo
o del ombligo

lo repito
no veo, no veo la hermosa ciudad
los bailarines de tango
los alrededores

no como asado
no vengo de lejos
pero soy bueno
y ciego.

never fished
desert
north of the roof
of the world
or its navel

let me repeat
i don't see, don't see the beautiful city
the tango dancers
the outskirts

i eat no asado
i do not come from afar
but i am good
and blind.

sangre natural

irreparar la mortalidad del agua
y mojarme
mojarme
mojarme
en tus ojos negros.

natural blood

unrepair water's mortality
and soak me
soak me
soak me
in your black eyes.

cajamarca

otorongo corre entre mis piernas aladas

gabriella grita
hay hongos, mamá
hay hongos grandes tóxicos, limpios, amarillos venenosos
cajamarca
las cenizas vivas

miro al amor en un balcón
la sierra verde
enjaulada en las iglesias limpias

una marca
en la caja
el oro
la gruta, siempre el oro

agüita caliente
para las penas gabriella dice
los pinos, mamá
abraza el árbol, mamá
abrázalo

dilo en inglés, mamá
para los canadienses

y vuelo como la mariposa roja
que siempre he querido ser
tengo las alas rotas

cajamarca

jaguar runs between my winged legs

gabriella screams
mushrooms, mamá
big toxic mushrooms, clean, yellow poisonous
cajamarca
the living ashes

i look at the love on a balcony
the green sierra
caged in clean churches

mark a
caja
the gold
the grotto, always the gold

hot hot water
for the pains
gabriella says
the pines, mamá
hug the tree, mamá
hug it

say it in english, mamá
for the canadians

and i flutter like the red butterfly
i've always wanted to be
my wings are broken

gabriella llora
me han roto mamá
quieren separarme de ti
los buscadores de oro
el alma de la abuela

pego las alas
suelto al otorongo
vomito los hongos
escupo el oro
y cajamarca se queda
llorando verde.

gabriella weeps
they've broken me mamá
they're trying to take me from you
the seekers of gold
grandmother's soul

i stick on the wings
release the jaguar
vomit the mushrooms
spit out the gold
and cajamarca remains
weeping green.

una pluma cae

A J. E. Eielson
I. M.

ni cuerpo
ni camisa

< *no far   no close*
            no south, no west >

la muerte es el trapecio exacto
el número del circo
en que nazca
es un lirio estrujado en mármol italiano

        la compostura de la epidermis peruana
se descascara en méxico en viena en milán

la arena es hielo
la palabra que condensa al cristal de la eternidad

        vuela en forma de colibrí sagrado.

il mio cuore non parla piú

a feather falls

For J. E. Eielson
I. M.

not body
not shirt

<no far   no close
                no south, no west>

death is a precise trapeze
the circus act
where it's born
an iris pressed in italian marble

        the composition of his peruvian epidermis
flayed in mexico in vienna in milan

the sand is ice
the word that condenses eternity's crystal

        flies in the form of a sacred hummingbird.

il mio cuore non parla piú

debería irme a vivir a colombia
he leído un poema escrito con colorete en una calle de medellín
he visto un ocaso fresco y encendido al mismo tiempo
un hombre negro mirando las manos blancas de alguien
un carro de agua
una loción que huele a flores calientes

y digo colombia
porque pienso en la palabra
y se me ocurren cosas en la boca
vidrio molido le llaman algunos
otra intención de silencio anaranjado
colibrí
plátano tierno
dientes de niña otra vez
arepas
un compás de cumbia
gorgojos en pasto

el recuerdo de la barba de un amigo que era profesor
una letra escrita con gomina
una frase que en otro país hubiera estado mal dicha
un cuadro amarillo que parece hecho de besos y caléndulas
una bala en la hoja del cuaderno

mi profesora de religión
era de colombia
se llamaba julia alba alba y julia
alba su rezo
y mi profesora de geografía era de medellín
se llamaba magdalena

i ought to go live in colombia
i once read a poem written in lipstick on a medellín street
i once saw a sunset that was both chilly and lit up
a black man looking at someone's white hands
a water car
lotion in a hot floral scent

and i say colombia
because when i think the word
things happen in my mouth
ground glass some call it
another motive for orange silence
hummingbird
green banana
baby teeth once more
arepas
cumbia beat
weevils in grass

the memory of the beard on a friend who was a teacher
a single letter written in hair gel
a sentence that would've been incorrect in another country
a yellow painting that looks like it's made of marigolds and kisses
a bullet atop a loose-leaf sheet

my religion teacher
was from colombia
her name was julia alba: daybreak and julia
daybreak her prayer
and my geography teacher was from medellín
her name was magdalena

el mundo, me decía
es un río, una ciudad pequeña
un chico bueno riéndose en la misa
un pan fresco en el momento exacto

y esas monjas se murieron, mientras subían un cerro
cubierto de hojas de limón
y esas monjas
aparecen a veces en la noche

debería irme a colombia.

the world, she told me
is a river, a little city
a good boy laughing at mass
fresh bread at exactly the right time

and those nuns died as they climbed a mountain
covered in lime leaves
and those nuns
appear sometimes at night

i ought to go to colombia.

el código cultural de la arena

para qué contar de sueños limpios
si ya todo está manchado por casas
rotas

la cama sin pies
la cama sin hijos
la cama muerta

aún bulle ese par de escenas
sin sentido
demasiados hombres en la
piel de cardo
hacer un solo hombre de mil

crear el silencio y a la vez
la palabra perfecta
que
como una tecla
bien apretada
diga
es aquí
se acaba el aire
y empieza
la tortuga
a desvestirse

solo un abrazo
bien dado
el oportuno
si bien dicho

the cultural code of the sand

why talk of clean dreams
when everything's been stained with broken
houses

bed with no feet
bed with no sons or daughters
lifeless bed

that pair of scenes still boils
senseless
too many men in
thistle skin
to make one man of a thousand

make silence and also
the perfect word
which
like a key
hard pressed
says
it's here
the air ends
and the turtle
begins
to disrobe

just a hug
a big one
the proper one
even so

la hipocresía milenaria
cae del caparazón

un plato con frejoles exactos
no puedo jugar más al alba buena
cuando se me cae la fealdad
por las orejas.

age-old hypocrisy
falls from the carapace

a plate of precise beans
i can no longer pretend to be the lovely daybreak
when ugly sloughs
from my ears.

manicura

pélame las uñas
las uñas pélamelas
o las manos destrózalas de una vez
rómpeme
están manchadas
con agujeros en los meñiques
los cantos mordidos
yemas cuajadas

he hecho caramelos de semen
con el pulgar y el índice
buscando manipular la existencia

he tocado la loza fría, loza de la muerte cerca de viena
ciudad sin uñas
en machu picchu he acariciado la faz de luna reflejada
y he amarrado a mis dedos el gras mojado
mojado de moco humanamente femenino

soy de agua y mis manos de agua se escurren
dedos descuidados
uñas que ya no existen
que no pueden rasgar guitarras

ni arañar el pecho de un hombre bueno
uno que crea en mis manos
entre rejas carcomidas, oxidadas
entre uñas comidas
vomitadas

soy sin manos
sin uñas para pintar.

manicure

peel my nails
my nails: peel them
or my hands, go ahead and wreck them
break me
they're splotchy
and have holes in the pinkies
chewed cuticles
curdled fingertips

i rolled caramels of semen
between my thumb and pointer
looking to manipulate existence

i touched cold pottery, death pottery near vienna
city of no nails
at machu picchu i stroked the reflected moon face
and to my fingers i fastened the wet grease
wet with humanly feminine mucus

i am from water and from water my hands are wrung
fingers untended
nails that no longer exist
and can't strum guitars

or claw the chest of a good man
one who believes in my hands
between rust-eaten grates
between nails eaten
vomited

i have no hands
no nails to paint.

poema de la distancia

si yo fuera eielson,
pintara un colibrí en tu lengua.

si has sentido alguna vez que hablas con la pared
que hablas con la pared
y recuerdos terribles de pajaritos muertos
y niñas amordazadas en zaguanes
repletos de gatos
apareándose como en un anime
muy sangriento, muy cruel

y que todo tu amor,
no es más que un vómito
que alguien pisa sin percatarse
de la humildad repentina en su zapato
y un muchacho bueno
te dice que no eres su tiempo
y corres por un pasaje enrejado de buenos aires
buscando otra melodía

un andar de procesión que
sea como un dedo intermitente
en el hueco más hondo de tu cuerpo
y no sabes cómo encender la luz
en los ojos de todos tus amigos
de toda tu familia que parece culparte de tantas desgracias
de los niños que mueren y
de los cuadros malpintados

si no sabes cómo pintar uvas en un bodegón
que reclama a gritos el espíritu de la embriaguez

poem on distance

if i were eielson,
i'd use your tongue to paint a hummingbird

if you've ever felt like you were talking to a wall
talking to a wall
and to terrible memories of dead birds
and girls gagged in vestibules
packed with cats
mating like in anime
incredibly bloody, incredibly cruel

and that all your love
was nothing more than vomit
someone stepped on heedless
of the sudden lowliness on his shoe
and a good guy
said you're not of his time
and you ran past a fenced buenos aires scene
seeking another melody

a processional gait like
an intermittent finger
in your body's deepest hole
and you don't know how to flick on the light
in the eyes of all your friends
of all the family who seem to blame you for the misfortune
of the dying children and
the sloppy paintings

if you don't know how to paint grapes in a still life
clamoring for intoxication's spirit

porque el escenario de nuestra locura y nuestra impotencia
es más grande y más hondo que todas las penumbras

si no hay luz zenital
ni trazo en la guarida plana
que solo ansía una nueva suerte y el esperma glorioso
se pierde en las mangas usadas de este siglo
lleno, lleno de basura

si no ves con ojos de la duda
la desesperación del cubismo
por qué hay liquen en el pelo
y cámaras escondidas
vigilando la historia, espiando dementes
las heladeras muertas de frío

es que falta amasar el pan
poner ajonjolí en la lengua de un caballo
pedir a un hombre que me bese la espalda sin darme cuenta
que mate a mi hermana
que haga justicia
a la niña que no he curado
y me devuelva la gloria
de ese grito interminable
que sale de mi coxis, de las cosas que no entiendo
de la constante negación de mi útero de elefante.

because the stage for our madness and impotence
is bigger and deeper than every shadow

if there's no zenithal light
or sketches in the level lair
longing simply for new luck
and glorious semen
is lost in the used sleeves
of this century
full, so full of trash

if you can't see with doubtful eyes
the despair of cubism
why there's lichen in your hair
and hidden cameras
keeping watch on history, spying demented
on fridges dead from cold

it's because someone has to knead the bread
put sesame on a horse's tongue
ask a man to kiss my back unbeknownst to me
to kill my sister
to do justice
to the girl i haven't healed
and restore me to the glory
of that endless shriek
emerging from my coccyx, from the things i don't understand
from the steady denial of my elephant uterus.

la rapsodia del tigre

no te das cuenta de quién soy, tigre. mimas mi vientre pensando en la repetición de tu linaje.
la nostalgia de los pueblos es sagrada, por eso la gente moderna necesita un uzquil.

respeta tigre la carne ajena.

tan lejos, observa. quién entra y sale de la cueva, quién viene y va de su casa. oscura casa de paredes altas. allí no entra un tigre, solo su alma.

la casa tiene un alma de tigre lamiendo los marcos de las ventanas, baboseando los baños y los balcones. el tigre anhela, el tigre desea, pero la mujer que habita los rincones solloza como niña asustada y dice vete alma de algo que ha inundado este lugar. el alma del tigre se enfurece y responde: inquilina bruta.

rhapsody of the tiger

you don't realize who i am, tiger. you coddle my belly and think about the
continuation of your line.
the peoples' nostalgia is sacred, this is why modern folks need an uzquil.

tiger, respect flesh that's not yours.

from afar, it observes. who enters and leaves the cave, who comes and
goes from its house. dark house, high walls. where no tiger can go, just its
soul.

the house has a tiger soul lapping at the window frames, slabbering bath-
rooms and balconies. the tiger yearns, the tiger desires, but the woman
who dwells in the corners sobs like a frightened child and says go away
soul of the thing that's flooded this place. the tiger soul is enraged and it
replies: stupid brute of a tenant.

sobre la igualdad

en el círculo, dulce círculo
de inmortalidad intensa

dónde ha quedado mi lejano país chino
el gran país de todos
donde no se repiten las caras

las voces son como un tambor que cambia la dirección de un río
la perspicacia de los cinco sonidos
cinco calles
cinco calamidades

la mirada occidental
siembra sus intenciones
ellos quieren llenar
la vacuidad china
con odio y desastres

el cascarón se ha roto
eso no era por amor, ni por ganar batallas
¿por qué una cruz de kiev
está flotando en un río sur americano?

es la moderna desesperación
quién está atado a quién
quién llora
esas olas ensangrentadas
de un océano pacífico en medio de un temblor
ya no me quiero mover
no quiero perros

on sameness

in the circle, sweet circle
of intense immortality

where my faraway chinese country stayed
the great country of all
where no faces repeat

the voices are like drums that reverse a river's flow
the keenness of the five sounds
five streets
five calamities

the gaze of the west
sows its intentions
wanting to fill
chinese vacuity
with disasters and hate

the eggshell has broken
not for love, or to win battles
why is a cross from kyiv
floating in a south american river?

this is modern despair
who's tied to whom
who weeps
those bloodstained waves
of a pacific ocean quaking
i don't want to move anymore
don't want dogs

no quiero sirvientes
no quiero la imaginación de una diosa sureña

el agua toma otros colores
los ojos de peter todavía me conmueven
algunos días con pavlo me hicieron muy feliz
y la esquina después de cuarenta y tres años
es la casa de los comienzos

la luz me parió en esta ciudad
y la odio también
quiero que mi mamá viva todas las vidas
quiero que mis hermanos sean niños otra vez.

or servants
don't want the imagination of a southern goddess

the water takes on other colors
peter's eyes still stir me
some days with pavlo made me happy
and the corner after forty-three years
is the house of beginnings

light birthed me in this city
and i hate it too
i want my mamá to live all the lives
i want my brother and sister to be children once again.

¿por qué tus diferencias
ahuyentan la vitalidad de mis músculos?
no soy la doncella fiel que parezco

quiero que me embarren con saliva
allí donde el cuerpo no sabe si florecer o morir
donde un tambor de áfrica reviente el danubio en mis tobillos

mi casa se engrandece cuando me reconozco
este cuero moreno
vivido entre piropos y lunas callejeras

quiero una guitarra celeste
no palabras rojas
eslavo, estoy cansada de ti
quiero al sol glaciar
de mi propia humanidad
despierta y al acecho

kiev quizás más limpia, tan celeste
como un mar de turquesas diluidas

tomo de este vino derramado
he muerto en tantas letras intraducibles

¿cómo es tu tierra?, valerosa. humana, puja como
aria, como judía, como gitana?, son las de allá
menos celosas. no cuentan las alverjas caídas
en el recogedor, no se calientan las nalgas
con el sol de enero.

why do your differences
dispel my muscles' vitality?
i am not the faithful maiden i appear to be

i want to be slathered in saliva
there were the body can't decide whether to bloom or die
where an african drum bursts the danube onto my ankles

my house balloons when i recognize myself
this dark hide
inhabited between catcalls and stray moons

i want a sky blue guitar
not red words
slav, i'm tired of you
i want the glacial sun
of my own humanity
awake, in wait

maybe kyiv is cleaner, so blue
like a sea of diluted turquoise

i drink of this spilled wine
i've died in so many untranslatable letters

what's your land like? valiant. human, striving like
an aryan, a jew, a gypsy? the women over there are
less jealous. they don't count the peas fallen
into the dustpan, don't warm their backsides
in the january sun.

no, no sé cómo me metí en este enredo de lenguajes,
una trenza de sílabas
un laberinto de emes, de pes, de dioses intrusos

no iré nunca a kiev, ni volveré a moscú.
lo prometo.

no, i don't know how i got caught in this tangle of language,
braided syllables
labyrinth of ems, pees, intrusive gods

i'll never go to kyiv, or go back to moscow.
i promise.

ángel de mi guarda

empiezo a sudar. tus alas se derriten desde mis ojos. escogiste alguna cavidad de mi cráneo y desde allí te vas haciendo agua.

¿en qué momento se vuelven invasores los aliados? ¿en qué momento dejo de pensar que los regalos son una bendición y que cada hermoso mantel, cada cortina, cada buen gesto no es más que una señal de erudición sobre mi simpleza, mi empequeñecido espectro?
te doy un bordado, una cuchara de madera, las tuyas tan desgastadas, no, no valen nada.

hormiga gris que cae y se levanta cien veces
lleva un grano de sal un ósculo de cobre
para alargarse íntimamente.
si las hormigas tuvieran espíritu de pez, el mundo de los huequitos que albergan sus huevos, serían peceras con escamas multicolores, algas, piedritas. pero las hormigas no se volverán peces, ni los peces, tigres, ni los tigres, dragones mitológicos. la hormiga caerá y se levantará cien veces.

me fascina la fotografía, eso me pone en desventaja frente a un ojo perturbado, me hace débil. inigualable lo que el vientre ve, la lejana oscuridad.

un fotógrafo tiene una inspiración en la hipófisis que va más allá de la sabiduría normal sobre las cosas. un fotógrafo puede condenarte por no saber mirar como él. encierra mucha muerte el ojo de un fotógrafo, quiere congelar el instante en que volteas el dedo, miras la calle, la luna se encarama, el suelo se moja, los amantes se dispersan, los bebés maman y las auroras boreales quedan pintadas en el firmamento. el ojo, como una hormiga captará lo necesario.

my guardian angel

i start to sweat. your wings drip from my eyes. you chose some cavity in my skull and are in there turning to water.

at what point do allies become invaders? at what point do i stop thinking of gifts as blessings and that every beautiful tablecloth, every curtain, every nice gesture is but a sign of erudition upon my simplicity, my narrowed spectrum?
i give you needlework, a wooden spoon, yours so worn, no, they're worthless.

gray ant that collapses and gets up a hundred times
carrying a grain of salt a copper osculation
just to intimately drag on.
if ants possessed fish spirits, the world of the holes that harbor their eggs would be aquariums with colorful scales, kelp, pebbles. but ants do not become fish, nor fish tigers, nor tigers mythical dragons. the ant will collapse and get up a hundred times.

i find photography fascinating, which puts me at a disadvantage when it comes to a disturbed eye, it makes me weak. unmatched, what the belly can see, the faraway dark.

photographers possess pituitary inspiration that goes beyond the normal wisdom of things. a photographer can condemn you for not knowing how to see the way they do. the eye of a photographer encloses a good deal of death; it wants to freeze the moment when you turn your finger, look at the street, the moon climbs up, the floor gets soaked, lovers disperse, babies nurse, and the aurora borealis is painted on the firmament. the eye, like an ant, snatches what's necessary.

un fotógrafo es un ser raro, hormiga y ángel al mismo tiempo. no mira las cosas como son sino que hace las cosas casi como él quisiera que fueran, y es tan importante el retrato, la imagen y el lenguaje del color, la distancia y el tamaño que se pueden descubrir todas las mentiras del universo con un solo enfoque. la voz de la noche se impregna en el papel, las despedidas, la frustración, las emociones, la vergüenza (sobre todo la vergüenza) y el orgullo (sobre todo el orgullo).

a photographer is a strange being, ant and angel all at once. they don't see things as they are, instead it's as if they make things into what they want, the image and language of color, distance, and size that can uncover the universe's every lie with a single shift of focus. night's voice permeates the paper, farewells, frustration, emotions, shame (above all, shame), and pride (above all, pride).

bodas de opio

miré sus ojos inferiores
negros, cansados
miré su corazón
y esa mancha de lozanía
hizo me
efímera, tardía, rancia y pasajera

llegamos al altar
con gran recogimiento
pido una ofrenda viviente
empiezo a toser, constipada
casi hasta quebrantarme
a sus pies

cóncavo
esperando el recibimiento
en cada segundo de muerte
de condena expiada
en la singular liturgia
sus manos estaban cerradas
como una puerta que tocas y tocas
pero no hay nadie del otro lado

yo llevaba un vestido negro,
muy bello con aberturas exageradas
a cada costado
él tenía un cardo muerto en el terno
en medio de una cortina de incienso
voz pausada, dijo
will be peace on earth

opium weddings

i looked into his low eyes
black, tired
i looked into his heart
and that splotch of vigor
made me
ephemeral, tardy, rancid, and fleeting

we arrive at the altar
in a state of absorption
i request a living offering
start to cough, phlegmy
till i've nearly smashed to pieces
at his feet

concave
awaiting the receiving
in each second of death
of an expiated sentence
in the singular liturgy
his hands closed
like a door you knock and knock on
but there's no one on the other side

i was wearing a black dress,
gorgeous with dramatic slits
on either side
he had dead thistle pinned to his suit
from within a curtain of incense
a voice said, unhurried
there will be peace on earth

yo me deshice en fiebre
y el gimió mientras corría hacia el río
soy juglar, mozo,
demasiado tierno
para el yugo del lar
y mientras corría hacia el río
los cardos cayeron de su solapa,
florecieron frente al retablo.

i broke into fever
and moaning he ran toward the river
i'm a minstrel, porter,
too tender
for the yoke of the hearth
and as he ran toward the river
the thistle fell from his lapel,
and bloomed in front of the retablo.

la guerra

1.

sentí que todos necesitaban hablar sobre aquellos días. la muerte ocupaba todavía sus conciencias y su tiempo. se sentaron alrededor de la mesa y sacaron fotografías en blanco y negro. para algunos era un recuerdo aterrador, para otros fue el ocaso necesario para empezar a vivir. recordaban a los rusos. de todos aquellos ancianos fue hilda la que me llamó la atención.

era una mujer hermosa. había pertenecido a la juventud nacional socialista sin reflexionar mucho si era políticamente correcto o no. su lozanía, frescura y belleza convivían en un conjunto armonioso y prometedor. era atlética y sagaz. se enamoró de un mecánico de aviones. él, sin embargo, había preferido a su prima regordeta y dependiente. ella sería la madre de sus hijos. hilda era muy locuaz y atractiva para rezagarla a los trabajos hogareños.

cincuenta años más tarde, hilda era una mujer triste y callada, de porte digno y excesivas buenas maneras. el viejo mecánico ya estaba muerto y su gorda y pausada viuda había hecho un infierno de su existencia. pero tenía hijos y nietos que la visitaban. incluso un bisnieto llamado paul.

de hilda quedaban rosas arregladas y una vajilla carísima sin tocar. ella tenía alzheimer, artritis y unos fríos ojos azules que se cansaban rápidamente como si no soportaran la luz.

me pidió que le ayudara a limpiar su casa todos los martes. y así fue. yo iba contenta porque la paga era insuperable, doscientos preciosos marcos por seis horas de trabajo durante las cuales no tenía que hacer mucho. de postre siempre había arroz con leche y compota de cerezas. era lo mejor del escueto almuerzo, constituido mayormente por una sopa de sobre o un panqué relleno de mermelada de aldi.

the war

1.

my sense was that everyone felt the need to talk about those days. death
still occupied their consciences and their time. they sat around the table
and pulled out black-and-white photographs. for some of them, it was
a terrifying memory, and for others, it was the twilight they needed to
begin living. they recalled the russians. of all the old folks, it was hilda
who i found most striking.

she was a gorgeous woman. she'd belonged to the youth branch of the
national socialist party and hadn't thought much about whether or not
it was politically correct. her vigor, freshness, and beauty coexisted in a
promisingly harmonious ensemble. she was athletic and clever. when she
fell in love with an airplane mechanic, he preferred her plump depend-
able cousin, who would be the mother of his children. hilda was too
chatty and attractive to be relegated to household chores.

fifty years later, hilda was a quiet, joyless woman, dignified in her bear-
ing and excessively well-mannered. the old mechanic had died, his heavy
sluggish wife having made his life a living hell. but she had children and
grandchildren who visited her. even a great-grandchild named paul.

all that remained for hilda were arrangements of roses and a very expen-
sive dishware set, untouched. she had alzheimer's, arthritis, and a pair of
cold blue eyes that tired easily, like they couldn't bear the light.

she asked me to help clean her house every tuesday, and that's what hap-
pened. i was happy to go because the pay was unbeatable, two hundred
precious marks for six hours of not very demanding work. for dessert
there was always rice pudding and cherry preserves. that was the best part
of the simple lunches, which mostly consisted of soup from a mix or a
pancake filled with jam from aldi.

hacía la limpieza en su casa durante mi día de franco en el asilo de ancianos. la hice durante casi dos años, hasta poco después de salir embarazada.

era una buena rutina. a las ocho de la mañana yo ya estaba en la puerta de su casa. en la sala, el piano descubierto, como si alguien hubiera estado tocando. al ver sus manos entumecidas y los dedos penosamente chuecos, solo podía adivinar que ella necesitaba acariciar las teclas. sobre la mesa de centro habían flores nuevas de alguna amiga que la visitaba, una caja de chocolates baratos y alguna revista de fácil lectura como selecciones, o frau, o geo en el mejor de los casos.

me invitaba un vaso de jugo de pera, hecho en alguna presa de granjeros ecologistas.

luego me pedía que le contara lo que había hecho durante la semana y ella poco a poco, casi por cucharadas soperas, también me iba contando la historia de su apuesto hermano quien cayera en la guerra. eso me gusta de la palabra *fallen* en alemán, que significa morir en el campo de batalla. *fallen*, es caerse. caerse. a veces sacaba los álbumes que estaban escondidos debajo de los muebles y mientras señalaba las fotografías color sepia de su uniforme con condecoraciones, suspiraba con una hondura acalambrante.

rudolf murió hace mucho en una guerra que ella no quería olvidar, porque el presente se le había quedado corto. se le escapó de las manos. ella también había muerto en esa guerra, pero no sé por qué razones torcidas del destino, su delgado cuerpo y su tierna voz seguían contando aquella historia, guardada en fotografías. es por el ciruelo, me dijo un día. me quede seguramente porque el ciruelo del jardín necesitaba que lo rieguen.

2.

¿tu abuelo murió en el campo de batalla? le pregunté a karl con cierto atrevimiento, yo sabía muy bien que a él no le gustaba tocar aquel tema.

i cleaned her house on my day off from the nursing home, for almost two years, until just after i got pregnant.

it was a good routine. by eight a.m. i was at her door. in the living room, the piano uncovered, like someone had just been playing it. when i saw her stiff hands with their painfully crooked fingers, i could only guess that she felt the need to stroke the keys. on the coffee table were fresh flowers from a friend who had visited, a box of cheap chocolates, and some easy-reading magazine like *reader's digest*, or *frau*, or at best *geo*.

she gave me a glass of pear juice pressed by eco-friendly farmers.

then she would ask me to tell her what i'd done that week and, little by little, by the tablespoon almost, she too would tell me things, the story of her handsome brother who had fallen in the war. i like this about the word "fallen" in german, which means to die on the battlefield. "fallen" is "caerse." "to fall." sometimes she pulled albums out from under the furniture and as she pointed at sepia photos of him in his uniform draped with medals, she would sigh deep cramp-inducing sighs.

rudolf died long ago in a war she didn't want to forget, because the present had come up short. it slipped out from between her fingers. she too had died in that war, but for some twisted reason of fate i didn't understand, her slim body and tender voice kept telling that story preserved in photos. it's because of the plum tree, she said one day. no doubt i stayed because the plum tree in the garden needed someone to water it.

2.
did your grandfather die on the battlefield? i asked karl somewhat boldly, knowing very well he didn't like to talk about it.

after, he replied. many years after, of stomach cancer. the war was just his excuse to stop taking care of himself and confront his own death. he was never in love with oma, but she was predictable. she could give him children.

después —contestó— mucho después, de cáncer al estómago. la guerra solo fue la excusa para empezar a descuidarse y enfrentarse con la idea de su propia muerte. él nunca estuvo enamorado de oma, pero ella era previsible. ella le podía dar hijos.

su gran amor fue mi tía hilda, pero él no se sentía capaz de cortejar a una mujer como ella. de hilda se podía prever que nunca tendría hijos. de mi oma se podía prever que, aunque sería mala madre, era una mujer que iba a necesitar los hijos. necesitaba además una casa, seguridad financiera, un jardín de hortalizas y un hombre al cual esperar.

tía hilda tenía un espíritu independiente, con su primer sueldo fue a conocer parís y luego roma, después vendrían sus viajes alrededor del mundo, incluso conoció a indira gandhi en delhi y a anwar sadat.

yo soy producto de unos anacoretas que se quedaron con sus ilusiones truncadas de aquella alemania anti judía. mi oma nunca entendió nada de política, tía hilda sí, y aunque sentía una aberración inmensa por lo que estaba pasando en los campos de concentración, ella no dudaba de su superioridad, su compostura y su weltanschaung como parte de los escogidos.

3.

me palpo la tremenda barriga. estoy esperando un hijo de karl. o una hija. nunca encontré mejor síntesis en mi vida que ser madre de este bebé por venir. pero me desespera la indiferencia de karl. su apatía. le hablo de la guerra porque se me ocurre que él también carga la pesada historia de su familia. lo quiero aliviar.

—te amo, le he dicho.

sus ojos azules, fríos y helados empiezan a quemar. me pregunto si él me está usando como un canal para perpetuar sus genes. los genes de una sarta de ancianos que aún viven entre bombardeos y rusos que violan a jovencitas. ellos no son de estos años, ellos no conocen a john lennon,

his true love was my aunt hilda, but he didn't feel capable of wooing a woman like her. it was clear hilda was never going to have children. as for my oma, it was clear that, even though she would be a bad mother, she was the kind of woman who would need children. she also needed a house, financial security, a vegetable garden, and a man to wait for.

aunt hilda had an independent spirit. with her first paycheck she went to see paris and then rome, later she took trips around the world, she even met indira gandhi in delhi and anwar sadat.

i'm the product of anchorites who were left with their shattered illusions of that anti-jewish germany. my oma never understood anything about politics. aunt hilda did, and even though she felt what had happened in the concentration camps was an enormous outrage, she didn't doubt her superiority, her composure, and her weltanschauung as one of the chosen.

3.
i feel my huge belly. i'm expecting karl's child. a son, or a daughter. never in my life have i felt a higher calling than becoming the mother of this baby that's on the way. but karl's indifference is disheartening. his apathy. i talk to him about the war because it occurs to me that he too is weighed down by his family's heavy history. i want to relieve his burden.

i love you, i've told him.

his blue eyes, cold, frozen, start to burn. i wonder if he's using me as a vehicle to carry on his genes. the genes of a line of old folks who still live among bombings and russians who rape young girls. they're not of this era, they don't know who john lennon is, or wonder why hendrix was black, or why there are so many hindu gurus, or why their beautiful grandson had to marry a woman who hovered somewhere between strange and alien, spawn of a faraway country that to them was exotic, backward. i am a small latin american woman who came to germany

ni se han preguntado por qué hendrix era negro, y por qué proliferan los gurús hindúes, ni por qué su hermoso nieto tuvo que casarse con una mujer a la que ven entre rara o ajena, engendro de un país lejano, exótico para ellos, atrasado. soy una pequeña mujer latinoamericana que vino terriblemente enamorada a alemania, donde el pasado se guarda en libros, revistas y fotografías (empolvadas en el peor de los casos), y no duerme ni deja dormir.

mi barriga es grande y pesa. he visto niños blancos y de ojos azules provenientes de madres mestizas como yo. todas pasean felices. alemania ofrece tantas facilidades para tener hijos. karl me ha pedido ir a visitar un campo de concentración donde su abuelo materno fue coronel. él también murió, de locura, hace apenas unos meses. karl se avergüenza de que su abuelo estuvo involucrado a favor de hitler. consciente del holocausto, mi hijo lo sabrá todo, me ha dicho. y yo siento que todo esto es una pesadilla y quisiera decirle que no voy. que quiero ir de compras, que me faltan camisetas y calzoncitos. que quiero adornar con muñecos el cuarto del bebé. y él ya ha reservado dos pasajes en el tren de primera clase a munich. nos quedaremos dos días allí y luego alquilaremos un auto para ir a auschwitz.

soy latinoamericana, le digo, no me importa tu guerra, quiero ser feliz, lo beso, descaradamente por toda la cara. y sus ojos azules son más azules, casi como un cristal de iglesia en invierno. pero lo amo tanto que sucumbo a su silencio, le cojo la mano, me pego a él, pongo su mano sobre mi inmensa panza y suspiro.

con el tiempo olvidará todo este rollo de querer revindicar las andanzas de su abuelo, con el tiempo se olvidará que es alemán y vivirá nomás . . . de repente hasta lo convenzo de irnos a vivir a españa, tenerife es lindo, hemos ido un par de veces de vacaciones. le rezo a la virgen todas las noches, le pido que haga algo por nosotros como pareja, para que mi hijo o hija no tenga que cargar con maldiciones, ni extrañas venganzas.

already terribly in love, with this country where the past is preserved in books, magazines, and photos (dusty ones, in the worst of cases), a past that hasn't gone to sleep and won't let you sleep either.

my belly is big and heavy. i've seen white blue-eyed children come from mestiza mothers like me. on their strolls they're all happy. germany makes it so easy to have children. karl has asked me to go on a visit to a concentration camp where his maternal grandfather was colonel. he died, of madness, just a few months ago. karl is ashamed of the fact that his grandfather was involved in the war on hitler's side. he'll be aware of the holocaust, my child will know everything, he's said. and to me it all feels like a nightmare and i want to tell him i'm not going. that i'm going shopping, i still need undershirts and underwear. that i want to decorate the baby's room with toys. and he's reserved two first-class train tickets to munich. we'll stay for two days and then rent a car to drive to auschwitz.

i'm latin american, i tell him, i don't care about your war, i want to be happy. i kiss him all over the face, shamelessly. and his blue eyes are even bluer, almost like a church window in winter. but i love him so much i succumb to his silence, i take his hand, lean into him, put his hand on my enormous belly and sigh.

eventually he'll forget all this chatter of wanting to vindicate his grandfather's choices, eventually he'll forget he's german and just live . . . maybe i'll even convince him to go live in spain, tenerife is lovely, we've gone a couple times on vacation. i pray to the virgin every night, ask her to do something for us as a couple, so my son or daughter won't have to shoulder a curse, or strange vengeances.

i don't want to find myself in a russian plaza, white carnations in hand, or weep over the helmets of unknown soldiers, i don't want to look for a jew to ask for forgiveness, i don't want to be part of this crime carried on through the lustra, in memory, in books, in art.

no quiero acabar en una plaza rusa llevando claveles blancos, llorar sobre cascos desolados desconocidos, no quiero buscar a un judío y pedirle perdón, no quiero ser parte de este crimen perpetuado a través de los lustros, en el recuerdo, en los libros, en el arte.

—estamos pagan do las consecuencias, y lo haremos bien, me asegura.

karl es sumamente cariñoso, me gusta cómo me abraza y me besa el pelo, pero me siento su instrumento, para una paz que busca por todas esas cosas que le metieron en la cabeza.

después que nazca el bebé iremos a polonia. hay una organización que apoya niños abandonados, podemos hacer que el bebé desde pequeño aprenda polaco. me parece una locura. pero, qué le puedo decir.

—mi amor, le digo, mi amor. la virgen, dios, jesús, nos perdonan todo.

cuando hablo así, karl me mira como imbécil. cree que soy una provinciana andina que solo necesita colmar el placer de sus sentidos y mandar un cheque a fin de mes a su familia amable y exageradamente condescendiente en algún valle lleno de maíz. me lo dice todo con su silencio y su mirada de sable, con esos ojos azules que a veces curan todo el mal y a veces proyectan una soledad maldita, que ni toda mi fe puede menguar.

sé que karl quiere tomar fotos cuando nazca el bebé. me incomoda un poco, tampoco me gustó cuando casi me exigió que me desvistiera a contraluz, para fotografiar mi perfil desnudo e hinchado sobre una bella pared clara como la luna. las fotos salieron espectaculares. escuché a un par de sus amigos que saben bastante de fotografía, que karl tenía una imaginería interna sobrenatural, genial, le dijeron y la técnica insuperable. yo me sentí una modelo rechoncha, con mi bebé pateando, tratando de complacer todas las necesidades lúdicas, expresivas y hasta sádicas de mi marido.

we're paying down the consequences, and we're going to do it right, he tells me resolutely.

karl is extremely affectionate, i like how he holds me and kisses my hair, but i feel like a tool in his search for peace through all the things they put in his head.

after the baby is born we should go to poland. there's an organization for abandoned children, we could have the baby learn polish starting from when he's little. it sounds crazy to me. but what can i say.

my love, i tell him, my love. the virgin, god, jesus, they forgive all.

when i talk like this, karl looks at me like i'm an idiot. he thinks i'm an andean provincial whose needs consist solely of satisfying the pleasures of her senses and sending a check at the end of the month to her nice, cartoonishly affable family in some corn-filled valley. he says it all with his silence and his saber gaze, with those blue eyes that sometimes heal everything that's wrong and other times project a cursed solitude that even all my faith can't diminish.

i know karl will want to take photos of the baby being born. it makes me a little uncomfortable, i didn't like it either when he practically demanded i undress, backlit, so he could photograph my naked swollen silhouette against a beautiful wall clear like the moon. the photos came out spectacular. i listened as a couple of his friends who know a lot about photography said karl's internal imagery was supernatural; genius, they told him, unbeatable technique. with my baby kicking, i felt like a pudgy little model, trying to please all the ludic, expressive, even sadistic needs of my husband.

it's cold, i said, after posing for over two hours. even as i occasionally wrapped myself in a jute blanket that was there, ready to warm me up, his strong will seemed to tell me, wordlessly, that i shouldn't even think about a break or moving without his direction.

hace frío, le dije, cuando estuve posando más de dos horas. aunque de vez en cuando me envolvía en una manta de yute que estaba dispuesta para entibiarme, su fuerte voluntad parecía decirme sin palabras que ni se me ocurriera un descanso o que me moviera donde él no lo indicara.

—quiero ir al baño, dije en algún momento.

mi pubis cubierto de abundante vello desde que estaba embarazada se erizaba con la temperatura, y con su álgida mirada detrás de los lentes intercambiables y los focos de luz blanca.

quisiera mandar al carajo, a karl y sus intenciones de belleza perpetuada en papel.

—no me siento bella, le dije. no creo que sean buenas fotos.

aunque creo que el bebé se alegrará de saber que ya desde el vientre era fotografiado, pienso, digo, ya no sé. a veces callo lo que tengo en mente para que él no haga ese rictus de desagrado y desaprobación que me hace sentir tonta y fuera de lugar. él continuó su trabajo hasta culminarlo.

igual que en el amor, igual que en todo lo que decide. insistió hasta conseguir los resultados deseados. recuerdo la libertad de las garzas, la arena suelta de las cinco de la tarde, cuando se avecina el viento que da la bienvenida a la noche. pienso en los perros callejeros de pacasmayo que siempre tienen que comer. pienso en mi hermano que no tiene profesión y sólo anda con la guitarra de peña en peña, buscando alegrar y alegrarse. nunca fijo, errante. envidio eso, la sal que no quiere salar los mejores guisos sino que se pierde al caer entre los dedos de un cocinero apurado.

sobre libertad de pobre quiero hablar, en medio de cuentos de guerra y conciencias precavidas. entre la culpa y el futuro prometedor de los seres que hacen bien las cosas, quiero escaparme con mi hijo o con mi hija a algún pueblo que quede a orillas del mar.

i want to go to the bathroom, i said at some point.

my pubis, covered in thick hair ever since i'd gotten pregnant, would sprout goosebumps when the temperature changed or when he cast a chilly gaze from behind those interchangeable lenses and white spotlights.

i wanted to tell them to go to hell, karl and his plans for beauty perpetuated on paper.

i don't feel beautiful, i said. the photos probably aren't any good.

though i think the baby would be happy to know he'd been photographed from the womb—i think, i say, i no longer know. sometimes i hush what's on my mind so he won't make that rictus of displeasure and disapproval that makes me feel stupid and out of place. he kept working until he was done.

like in love, like in everything he decides on, he insisted until he'd gotten the desired results. i remember the freedom of the herons, the loose five o'clock sand, the approach of the wind that ushers in the night. i think about pacasmayo's stray dogs, always in need of something to eat. i think about my brother, who has no job and simply walks from peña to peña with his guitar, looking to make happiness and be happy. never fixed, roving. i envy that, salt that doesn't wish to salt the best stews, but would rather be lost from between the fingers of a hurried cook.

amid stories of war and cautious consciences what i want to talk about is the freedom of the poor. between blame and the promising future of those beings who do things right, i wish to slip away with my son or my daughter to some town on the shores of the sea.

madness on the highest building

do you think am i happy with this kiss on my mouth?
do you think am i trusty with quick bitches giving pleasure in
the next room?
it's not the pleasure, are not the bitches
it's the strange sound, i'm becaming part of a dirty wall
the ceilings are falling
i'm drinking mate

do you think am i glad with this language?
yo solo pienso en español, pero no puedo decir qué pienso
do you think am i happy with the place i was born
the dust is still covering the streets of my brain
solo veo el cerro, solo el cerro

do you think it's enough pain to run away?
yo defiendo la cruz, la sangre, ser la última, la no vengada, la
        pisoteada
no more sadism, the porno stars, the media lies, the pictures of
war in the middle east
do you think have i seen enough pictures of destructed lifes?
scarfaces on the church's corner

vivo cerca de un hermoso pasaje llamado "la piedad"
do you think it's old and historical enough
to be part of this city story?

hablo un lenguaje mezclado de imágenes
niet
someone says god is hidden only in the perfect language
the language is the city
the city must be burned
estoy en medio del fuego y escribo en tu boca

madness on the highest building

do you think am i happy with this kiss on my mouth?
do you think am i trusty with quick bitches giving pleasure
in the next room?
it's not the pleasure, are not the bitches
it's the strange sound, i'm becaming part of a dirty wall
the ceilings are falling
i'm drinking mate

do you think am i glad with this language?
i only think in spanish, but i can't say what i think
do you think am i happy with the place i was born
the dust is still covering the streets of my brain
i only see the mountains, just the mountains

do you think it's enough pain to run away?
i defend the cross, blood, coming in last, the unavenged, those
    crushed underfoot
no more sadism, the porno stars, the media lies, the pictures of
war in the middle east
do you think have i seen enough pictures of destructed lifes?
scarfaces on the church's corner

i live near a lovely pasaje called "la piedad"
do you think it's old and historical enough
to be part of this city story?

i speak a language mixed with images
niet
someone says god is hidden only in the perfect language
the language is the city
the city must be burned
i am in the middle of the fire and i write in your mouth

me escondo bajo tu axila
pueden rusia y kiev defenderme de estos malhechores

i don't want to pay taxes
i don't want to charge for cooking a plate of ceviche
drinking pisco sour, peruvian style
it's that from chile or from perú? same clear drug

oh, i forgot that
i was eating apple candies between java and paris
am i happy being a cosmopolitan whore?
i never sell sex, i sell words

te vendo el paraíso, verde, para turismo promiscuo
all the nations together
one hundred rooms, one hundred ways to fuck
a picture of an argentinian novelist on a china wall

am i good enough to be a mother?
esta noche, paris en mi cama, recuerdo un amante francés en
nueva york
do i have enough stories to write the sky with new beginnings?

the emptiness is full
i run to the toilet
do i have enough friends to let them die with my stories?
no, no soy como vargas llosa

do i need to say i'm peruvian, with little, little indian blood?
the chinese kitchen, ahh . . . we forget that for now!
but i miss so much a good played condor pasa
pasa condor, pasa
borra esta mierda, bórrala con tus alas sagradas.

i hide in your armpit
can russia and kyiv defend me from these evildoers

i don't want to pay taxes
i don't want to charge for cooking a plate of ceviche
drinking pisco sour, peruvian style
it's that from chile or from perú? same clear drug

oh, i forgot that
i was eating apple candies between java and paris
am i happy being a cosmopolitan whore?
i never sell sex, i sell words

i sell you paradise, green, for promiscuous tourism
all the nations together
one hundred rooms, one hundred ways to fuck
a picture of an argentinian novelist on a china wall

am i good enough to be a mother?
tonight, paris in my bed, i remember a french lover in
new york
do i have enough stories to write the sky with new
     beginnings?

the emptiness is full
i run to the toilet
do i have enough friends to let them die with my stories?
no, i'm not like vargas llosa

do i need to say i'm peruvian, with little, little indian blood?
the chinese kitchen, ahh . . . we forget that for now!
but i miss so much a good played condor pasa
pass, condor, pass
erase this shit, erase it with your sacred wings.

chernobyl kid

hey, debajo del seno derecho tengo herpes
duele la lengua
y el pie derecho también
allí donde pisé baba de perro
en una calle agujereada

¿cómo se llama esa gran ciudad?
no me acuerdo del hombre
ni del beso
¿era rubio?
¿de ojos amarillos?
¿de piel de escama de pez de rana?

tengo una bomba en el pecho
quiere explotar
hinchar de dolor más dolor
un verano insoportable

y en algo somos parecidos
respiro el peor aire
aquí en este hemisferio
sin esperanza, sin abrazo

eso es
tan terrible como
la radiación
o la bomba h.

chernobyl kid

hey, under my right breast i have herpes
my tongue hurts
and my right foot too
there where i stepped on dog slobber
on a potholed street

what's the name of that great city?
i can't remember the man
or the kiss
was he blond?
with yellow eyes?
with scaly skin like a fish like a frog?

i have a bomb in my chest
eager to explode
to swell with pain more pain
an unbearable summer

and in one way we're alike
i breathe the worst air
here in this hemisphere
with no hope, no embrace

it's as
terrible as
radiation
or the h bomb.

quiero matar a mi hermana
su peso sobre mí
ah, su peso sobre mí

hila hebras antiguas
crisantemos en el pecho de la arena
muy-muy
pequeña niña bizca
no ha podido defenderse sola

ella soporta los miles de kilómetros
erguida
entre banderines de satén
iiiiiiiiiiak
rompe el codo que no deja
abrir la mano para el éxtasis

tomo té en mi pequeña taza
ella alienta a los dragones
respira y reconoce
su superioridad:
destruyan a la pequeña
despójenla

y yo le mendigaría copos azules
en mi bolsa de plástico de hermana menor y mendiga

o que se muera
o que se muera.

i want to kill my sister
her weight on me
oh, her weight on me

she spins ancient thread
chrysanthemums in the sand's chest
mui-mui
little wall-eyed girl
couldn't defend herself on her own

she withstands the thousands of kilometers
upright
between satin pennants
iiiiiiiiiiak
breaks the elbow that won't let her
open her hand to ecstasy

i sip tea in my little cup
she urges on the dragons
takes a breath and recognizes
her superiority:
destroy that little girl
strip her

and i would beg her for blue corn flakes
in my plastic baggie, little beggar sister

or let her die
or let her die.

poem for georg trakl

der mensch, das dunkel tier
eso significa más o menos que yo mujer
medio leona
medio bestia

a pesar de los zapatos comprados en escaparates
tengo un pesar inmenso en mi tráquea

i wish i could be a lioness
i girl without shame
i wish i could eat
all the russian soldiers
a war i never met

cocino gallinas mientras miro pomos azules
y deshojo plantas de ajíes
y busco en la melena antigua
de mi animal hembra inventado
que escapa en las noches
y succiona leche de luna

ich möchte dieser frieden
der nur nach dem kampf kommt

ich moechte ein messer unter mein bettkissen
und der mond im stuecken schneiden

quiero volar, como las moscas
no, no, mejor como las aves rapaces
no, mejor como las abejas o los chanchos
no, mejor como las águilas norteamericanas

poem for georg trakl

der mensch, das dunkel tier
that means, more or less, that i, woman
half lioness
half beast

despite the shoes purchased from shop windows
have an enormous sorrow pressing on my trachea

i wish i could be a lioness
i girl without shame
i wish i could eat
all the russian soldiers
a war i never met

i cook chicken while gazing at blue knobs
and shuck ají plants
and search the ancient mane
of my invented female animal
who escapes at night
and sucks on moon milk

ich möchte dieser frieden
der nur nach dem kampf kommt

ich moechte ein messer unter mein bettkissen
und der mond im stuecken schneiden

i want to fly, like bluebottles
no, no, more like raptors
no, more like bees or hogs
no, more like north american eagles

no, no . . . mejor
como un piloto de avión
compadeciendo mi desgracia

no, no . . . more
like an airplane pilot
pitying my misfortune

madre e hija

voy a figurarme otra belleza sin vacíos, le he preguntado, ¿somos así?,
como esa madre y esa hija que se amistan y se distan, se contemplan,
se desvelan, alegres, tristes, se consuelan, somos espejo de este tiempo
moderno, los *shopping malls*, las barbies, los programas de teve con
humor ácido, azul, amargo o amarillo de los simpsons, somos parte de
la iglesia donde rezamos sin creer literalmente en esos dioses condena-
dos a estar quietos, somos el incienso de la mañana comprado en la ave-
nida corrientes, el azar de la alegría, en una ciudad, que un día nos ama y
otro nos expulsa, somos sus muñecas, su pony de peluche, el pingüino de
temaiken, el canguro que te regaló pablo. somos los libros que no puedo
publicar, los que he regalado, los que aún quedan debajo de la cama,
somos esos libros que me desvelan, los que me da miedo leer, porque
reconocería mis 45 pecados capitales, mis miedos, mis marañas, mis ape-
gos, mi lujuria, somos ese vino que se queda en la mesa sin tomar por mi
acidez estomacal, el yogur bebible que dejas a la mitad, somos el recuerdo
de aquel viaje a tijuana, el idioma del abuelo que queremos aprender jun-
tas, ¿cómo se dice cielo en chino mamá? y cómo se construye una pirá-
mide como la de quintanarró, somos las seis de la mañana, la planta de
ají caída al pasaje, una dupla que no encaja en ninguna parte, la eterna
excusa de pasear y vagar por la vida, el rechazo de los fuertes, la locura de
la curiosidad, somos el recuerdo de la abuela, las llamadas a escondidas,
mamá vivirás hasta que volvamos y podamos achicarnos a tu lado, cami-
nar despacito, volvernos un grano de loc-tao, una cucharada de maicena,
somos propensas a dejarnos llevar por la tecnología, a amar en exceso,
caernos, a herirnos, a recordar alemania, los huevos de chocolate en un
jardín suabo, somos constantes en la esperanza, volubles en la creación,
propensas al llanto, buscamos un amante espiritual que nos resuelva los
terribles acertijos, de la soledad y el desarraigo, buscamos amigos en las
escuelas, las clases de yoga, los turistas; hemos malamado a un fotógrafo,
un escritor, un drogadicto, un bebedor desmedido, hemos amado más

mother and daughter

i'm going to imagine another beauty with no gaps, i've asked her, is that
what we're like? like that mother and daughter who grow close then apart,
contemplate each other, keep each other up, happy, sad, comfort each
other, we're a mirror for this modern time, the malls, the barbies, the tee-
vee shows with their acid humor, blue, bitter, or simpsons yellow, we're
part of that church where we pray without literally believing in those
gods condemned to stillness, we're morning incense bought on avenida
corrientes, joy's coincidences, in a city that loves us one day and expels
us the next, we're its dolls, its stuffed pony, the penguin at temaikèn zoo,
the kangaroo pablo gave you. we're the books i can't publish, the ones
i've given away, the ones still under the bed, we're the books that keep me
up, the ones i'm afraid to read, because i would recognize my 45 cardinal
sins, my fears, my tangles, my inclinations, my lust, we're the wine sitting
on the table, untouched because i have heartburn, the yogurt drink you
leave half-finished, we're the memory of that trip to tijuana, your grandfa-
ther's language that we want to learn together, how do you say sky in chi-
nese mamá? and how do they make pyramids like the one in quintana
roo, we are six in the morning, the ají plant fallen into the passageway, a
duo that doesn't fit in anywhere, the eternal excuse of strolling and roam-
ing through life, rejecting the strong, the madness of curiosity, we're the
memory of your grandmother, the secret phone calls, mamá you'll live
until we can come back and grow small at your side, walk slowly, turn
into a luk tau bean, a spoonful of cornstarch, we're prone to getting swept
away by technology, to loving in excess, falling, getting hurt, remember-
ing germany, chocolate eggs in a swabian garden, we hold steady in our
hope, fickle in creation, prone to tears, we look for a spiritual lover who
can solve our terrible riddles, about solitude and rootlessness, we look
for friends at school, in yoga classes, among tourists; we've misloved a
photographer, a writer, a drug addict, a disproportionate drinker, we've
felt more love for a family member free like a miracle, like foam we can't

a una pariente libre como un milagro, como espuma que no se deja aga-
rrar y hemos roto los modelos y ahora estamos enardecidas de espacio y
buscamos unas alas que nos eleven, un huracán que nos haga recordar la
fuerza divina, una oración de un padre amante a la distancia.

grasp, and we've broken models and now we're inflamed with space and looking for wings to raise us, a hurricane to remind us of divine strength, a prayer from a loving father in the distance.

cerca del río

todavía creo que podré retroceder en el tiempo, no entrar al agua, evitarlo. todavía pienso en ese día como si hubiera sido ayer, la temperatura del agua, lo siento todo, la frescura en mi cuerpo caliente. todavía creo que hubiera podido decir no, no me voy a bañar. en la cama de la clínica repasaba los hechos. nuestra partida de passau en bici, claudia y yo estábamos sumamente entusiasmadas, gehard se sentía responsable por las dos.

son 800 kilómetros chicas, nos dijo. miré a claudia, ella se veía más contenta. en los últimos meses no había hecho nada extraordinario, de su casa al trabajo, de compras, al café . . . ese viaje a austria fue preparado y esperado con antelación. gehard revisó las bicicletas meticulosamente. llevó herramientas, nos entrenó para cualquier percance, para manejar bajo la lluvia. gehard ya tenía más de 3000 kilómetros de pedalear por distintos países en europa.

tomamos un *ferry* en passau y la aventura comenzó, no me cabía el corazón en el pecho. au, como duele, *es tut weh* . . . le dije a la enfermera. *schon gut*, me dijo ella y me miró con compasión, mi cara morena y amarilla, más pálida, sin comer una semana, el suero, la operación todo tan rápido. movió la cabeza negativamente. yo ya no podía llorar.

si hubiera nacido se llamaría julián, me gustaba ese nombre, nunca lo había escuchado en perú, en la escuela de alemania sí, el hijo de la profesora de francés se llamaba julián. si hubiera nacido, hubiéramos ido a viena juntos. me quedé en melk, a 70 kilómetros de viena, nunca llegamos. me operaron en esa clínica y el doctor me dijo que el esfuerzo físico había sido demasiado. necesitaría un par de meses para recuperarme. iba a la capilla todos los días y ya no lloraba. no me daba pena, porque no hubiera sabido que hacer con un niño en aquel tiempo, no hubiera sabido como criarlo, yo quería conocer europa, todo todo el mundo, también a sus hombres. si hubiera nacido se hubiera llamado julián.

by the river

i still believe i could go back in time, not get in the water, avert it. i still think about that day as if it were yesterday, the temperature of the water, i feel it all, the coolness on my hot body. i still believe i could have said no, i'm not going swimming. from the clinic bed i went over the events. our departure from passau on bikes, claudia and i extremely excited, gehard feeling responsible for us both.

800 kilometers, girls, he said. i looked at claudia, she seemed happier. for the past few months she hadn't done anything out of the ordinary, from home to work, from groceries, to the café . . . the trip to austria had been preplanned and much anticipated. gehard checked the bikes carefully. he brought tools, we trained for all possible mishaps, learned to bike in the rain. gehard had more than 3,000 kilometers pedaling all over europe under his belt.

in passau we got on a ferry and began our adventure, my heart leaping out of my chest. ow, it hurts so much, *es tut weh* . . . i told the nurse. *schon gut*, she said, and looked at me pityingly, my brown and yellow face, paler, a week without food, the iv, the operation all so fast. she shook her head. i could no longer cry.

if he had been born i would've named him julián, a name i liked, i'd never heard it in peru, but at my german school, the son of the french teacher was named julián. if he'd been born, we would've gone to vienna together. i stayed in melk, 70 kilometers from vienna, we never arrived. i had my operation at the clinic and the doctor told me the physical strain had been too much. i would need a couple months to recover. i went to the chapel every day and did not cry. it didn't make me sad, because i wouldn't have known what to do with a child in those days, i wouldn't have known how to raise one, i wanted to see europe, the whole world, and its men too. if he'd been born his name would've been julián.

el agua del danubio es muy fría, helada, aún en verano. terrible inunda la piel, los huesos, las glándulas, se come vivo lo que lleva uno adentro. cuando era muy chica tocaba el piano y la única pieza que podía tocar perfectamente sin leer la partitura era "el danubio azul". en aquel entonces nunca pensé que me metería al contaminado río danubio, 70 kilómetros antes de llegar a la ciudad soñada, a la ciudad esperada y dejar tantas lágrimas, me siento responsable por el río.

hay una canción de billy joel que se llama "vienna", dice, *vienna waits for you* . . .
supongo que si julián hubiera nacido, me acompañaría a visitar la casa de hundertwasser. hay una capilla en melk, donde una virgen silenciosa parece observar, no habla, porque no podría contar de todo el dolor que uno deja allí, me imagino que muchas personas se retuercen en esas bancas de pesar o de agradecimiento por la vida. para consolarme pienso que julián está en el cielo y dice: *vienna waits for you*.

the waters of the danube are very cold, freezing, even in summer. terrible, flooding your skin, bones, glands, eating your insides alive. when i was little i played piano and the only piece i could play perfectly without looking at sheet music was "the blue danube." back then i would've never imagined that one day i would enter the polluted danube river, 70 kilometers before arriving at the city of my dreams, the city i'd anticipated for so long, and shedding so many tears, i feel responsible for the river.

there's a billy joel song called "vienna," the lyrics go, *vienna waits for you . . .*
i suppose if julián had been born, he would've come with me to visit the hundertwasser house. there's a chapel in melk, where a silent virgin seems to watch, unspeaking, because she couldn't possibly recount all the pain that gets left there, i imagine a lot of people twist on those benches in remorse or gratitude for life. to make myself feel better i imagine julián in heaven and he says: *vienna waits for you.*

mujer comida por gatos

uno por uno alguien come mis ojos, me va sacando la carne de las orejas, se mete dentro de mi pecho, me saca el corazón. deben ser pelos los que siento sobre la piel. pelillos y también rasguños leves; me desangro, siento la lengua de un ser y unos dientes pequeños. es simultáneo, va por todo el cuerpo, en la cara, en el cráneo, los pies, la barriga, los pechos. toda yo cubierta por pisaditas diminutas. una cosa: no duele, ni hace cosquillas; solo eso. los latidos de cuatro patas embargándome, delirantes.

no sé como vine a parar a esta habitación, no sé como caí inconsciente y ellos se permitieron arremeter sobre mí. empezaron a devorarme, de a poquitos. mordisco tras mordisco, lamida tras lamida. ya no tengo nariz, hay un hueco. ni tráquea. hay otro hueco.

debo haber vivido sola en esta casa horrible, alguien me abandonó, dejó que ellos se apoderarán de todo.

la vecina es de tucumán. la vecina me odia. ha tapiado la ventana. no entra luz, todo está oscuro, me ha encerrado. ella se cree dueña de la luz. ella crió a los gatos, luego ellos vinieron a mi casa.

después caí, sedienta, sin luz. la vecina debe estar feliz. no tengo labios. no había nadie quien me bese.

no tengo frío ni calor. alguien debería decirle a la vecina que abra la ventana.
así los gatos regresarían por donde vinieron.

woman eaten by cats

someone is eating my eyes one by one, stripping the flesh from my ears, climbing into my chest, pulling out my heart. those must be whiskers i'm feeling on my skin. little whiskers and light scratches too; i bleed, feel somebody's tongue and tiny teeth. it's simultaneous, all over my body, on my face, scalp, feet, stomach, chest. all of me covered in soft footfalls. one thing: it doesn't hurt, or tickle; that's all. the beating of four delirious paws, overwhelming me.

i don't know how i ended up in this room, don't know how i fell unconscious as they rushed forward. they began to devour me, little by little. nibble by nibble, lapping at me. i no longer have a nose, it's a hole. nor a windpipe. another hole.

i must've lived alone in this horrible house. someone abandoned me, and let them seize everything.

my neighbor is from tucumán. my neighbor hates me. she's bricked up the window. there's no light, everything is dark, she's closed me in. she thinks she owns the light. she raised the cats, and then they came to my house.

and then i fell, parched, lightless. my neighbor must be happy. i have no lips. there was no one to kiss me.

i am not hot or cold. someone should tell my neighbor to open the window.
that way the cats will leave the way they came.

Translator's Afterword

A few years ago, I asked a translator who had been immersed in academia for many years if she saw differences in how academics approached translation versus how working translators did. (The line between the two is often blurred; sometimes both labels apply to the same person.) She told me that literary critics and reviewers often approach translation at the level of the sentence, whereas translators work at two levels: with the sentence, yes, but also with the whole work.

That idea has stuck with me. It returns to me when, reading as an editor, I ponder a translation choice that has given me pause—only to see how it reappears, transfigured, later in the text, evidence of a word that echoed across pages in the original and that the translator has worked to preserve the echoes of in their translation. This is not to say that those moments of semi-strangeness introduced via a desire to retain a text's echoes always merit keeping. There have been many times that an editor reading one of my translations pointed out a snag in the fabric of the text and helped me realize that actually, it made more sense to change up how I'd translated a repeated word in order to let it rise to the occasion of its local context, its sentence.

As I was re-reading *A Blind Salmon* at the level of the whole work, I was again struck by the many echoes Julia has woven into this collection— or poemario, a Spanish word I have often wished had a neater equivalent in English than the comparatively unwieldy "poetry collection." Jorge Eduardo Eielson, the Peruvian poet and visual artist who died in Milan as Julia was writing these poems in Buenos Aires, makes a couple appearances. (His poemario *Room in Rome*, translated by *A Blind Salmon*'s editor

Shook, is a revelation—fortuitous echoes from behind the scenes of this book.) The word "osculation" ("ósculo") appears twice—a word I learned in English thanks to this poemario and recently used to win a round of the word game "Ghost." Thistle and flaying and elderly German women and the urge to kill one's sister echo. Chewed nails also echo across the collection, in one instance echoing in a more literal way a word in a nearby line: "entre rejas carcomidas, oxidadas / entre uñas comidas / vomitadas" in "manicura" or "manicure." In my translation, I mimic the sonic echo between the words "carcomida" and "comida" by translating those lines as "between rust-eaten grates / between nails eaten / vomited."

Tigers echo, and even reach a photo of a character in Kenya. Julia and I chatted about this moment after I noted that tigers are native to Asia, and there are no wild tigers in Africa. For a few drafts, the photo in that poem featured Reiner standing next to a lion, not a tiger, in my translation. But after reviewing the poems as a poemario, I changed it back to "tiger," an image that accrues weight in the collection through repetition.

One big, resounding echo is evident just from this translation's table of contents—the two poems titled "on sameness." In the original poemario, "on sameness" is Julia's self-translation of "sobre la igualdad," which I've rendered in my translation as the second "on sameness." I must've read Julia's self-translation at some point as I was reading the whole collection, but when it came time to make my own translation of "sobre la igualdad," I made sure Julia's had been cleared from my head. In general, I try not to read others' translations of a work before writing my own, leery as I am of stowaway turns-of-phrase that I might pull out without realizing they are someone else's words.

Looking at the two un-same poems entitled "on sameness" side by side, I notice that they open the same way, with "in the circle, sweet circle / of intense immortality," Julia and I arriving independently at the same two lines in English. Julia's "anger and cruel desires" in stanza four made me revisit the Spanish I worked from to in turn revisit my rather banal

"disasters and hate." The differences in where the lines break across the two poems occasioned more revisiting. The ending line of Julia's version, where she references the potrero de Santa Rosa by name (another poema-rio-level echo) makes clear that the poem shifted between the version she translated from (or revised in English) and the poem in Spanish I translated, which ends simply with "quiero que mis hermanos sean niños otra vez," no mention of the potrero (which Julia once described to me as a piece of farmland smaller than the "chacras" I am more familiar with and that bilingual dictionaries render as "pasture" or "paddock").

You might have noticed that the first "on sameness" is rendered in a different typeface than the second "on sameness" and the surrounding translations. This was our answer to the question of a thoroughly multilingual collection. In the original, the borders between Julia's Spanish and Julia's English were clearer, given that they were the commonly agreed-upon borders between languages; in this translation, the borders between Julia's English and my English would have been less clear without some visual cues. With our respective Englishes denoted typographically, I hope you too can see the way Julia's and my Englishes echo each other, sometimes within the same poem—and also speak to each other, echoing the conversations we have via sound wave over video chat.

Now would be the place for a segue into the exploration of echo as metaphor for translation, but I will keep myself from falling into that pool of water. Though I, echo-tracer and maybe thus Echo, spend a lot of time gazing upon the original, the original—and its author—also gaze back at me, and I have agency in this exchanging of letters ("de emes, de pes, de dioses intrusos" / "of ems, pees, intrusive gods"). There are parts of the exchange where Julia and I are probably more or less on level ground, though coming from different directions, if there are even ways of measuring such things—say, in Julia's and my relationships to "the land with no owners / the face is not repeating itself" (Julia's English) or "the great country of all / where no faces repeat" (my English). There are also parts of this exchange that are weighted toward me, possessing as I do not just

"the west eye," "the gaze of the west," but also wider, more uncontested access to English—which is so rich as a language and can also so easily flatten, on the page and through the encounters it mediates. As Jhumpa Lahiri puts it in her meditation on translation as Echo, in *Translating Myself and Others*, "Though Echo's hunt ends in failure, she helps us to better appreciate the translator's contradictory role as someone who both comes second and exercises a certain degree of power in the course of wrestling a text into a new language." In wrestling, I exercise my agency in rendering the "mamá" in "sobre la igualdad" not as "mother" but as "mamá," a choice Julia and I have discussed in my translations of other work by her; I exercise my agency in any number / all of the choices in the English translation. I exercise power through the medium of English, which is often both portal and maw.

I could've rendered the "igualdad" in the title of "sobre la igualdad" as "equality" instead of "sameness." I do not claim that *A Blind Salmon* is "equal" to Julia's *Un salmón ciego*, or vice versa. I certainly cannot claim that it is the same, as the very poems "on sameness" would give the lie to that assertion. But what I can tell you is that there are two: two of us Sino diasporans, two people who speak Spanish and English and other languages too, two books published in two discrete zones in time and space. You can count them on or between your hands: here is the one, and here is the other. Two, now together.

Translator's Acknowledgments

With gratitude to Shook and Gwen for plunging into this work with me, and always to Julia for the conversations, the generous collaboration, and the poems themselves.

Gratitude as well to editors who have given these poems homes: An earlier version of "gabriella sleeps" was published by Steve Halle in *Spoon River Poetry Review*, and earlier versions of "the desert dispels" and "woman eaten by cats" were published by Suzi F. Garcia in *Poetry*.

Biographical Information

Born into a tusán (Chinese Peruvian) family in Chepén, Peru, **Julia Wong Kcomt** is the author of eighteen volumes of poetry, seven books of fiction, and three collections of hybrid prose. In English, her work has been published in *The Margins*, *McSweeney's*, *Poetry*, and other outlets. She currently lives between Lima and Lisbon.

Jennifer Shyue is a translator from Spanish. Her translations include Julia Wong Kcomt's chapbook *Vice-royal-ties* and Augusto Higa Oshiro's novel *The Enlightenment of Katzuo Nakamatsu*. She can be found at shyue.co.